NAOMI MAHER.

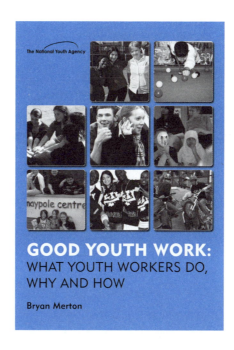

GOOD YOUTH WORK:
WHAT YOUTH WORKERS DO, WHY AND HOW

Bryan Merton

Published by

The National Youth Agency

Eastgate House,
19–23 Humberstone Road,
Leicester LE5 3GJ.
Tel: 0116 242 7350. Fax: 0116 242 7444.
E-mail: nya@nya.org.uk
Websites:
www.nya.org.uk
www.youthinformation.com

Text may be photocopied free of charge for educational and training purposes. Enquiries concerning reproduction outside these terms should be addressed to the publisher.

The NYA is grateful to the Department for Children, Schools and Families for its support of this project.

© The National Youth Agency, August 2007
ISBN: 978 0 86155 341 9
Price: £8.50

Design and Layout: Jim Preston, The National Youth Agency
Printed in the UK by Spectrum Printing Services Limited, Leicester

AN EXPLANATION OF WHAT YOUTH WORKERS DO, WHY AND HOW

Contents

Introduction	1
The 3 (or 4) Rs	3
Resourcefulness	3
Resilience	7
Resolve	9
Opportunities and risks	11
A safe place	19
A reflective space	20
Activity and achievement	25
Choice and voice	26
Responding to the here and now	28
The qualities and skills of youth workers	31
Last words	38
Notes	40

GOOD YOUTH WORK:

About the author

Bryan Merton MA, PGCE and BA (Hons) is an independent consultant. He is visiting professor at the Youth Affairs Unit, De Montfort University, senior consultant and research associate at the National Institute for Adult Continuing Education, and consultant to The National Youth Agency. From 1984–96 he was a member of HM Inspectorate for Schools and became the staff inspector responsible for the youth, adult and continuing education team. He was until recently senior consultant to the NIACE/NYA Young Adults Learning Partnership.

Bryan has written and taught extensively on informal learning and its contribution to countering social exclusion and has published his work in books and professional journals. He is committed to improving the quality of services for young people in their local communities and to exploring innovative responses to enduring social policy challenges.

AN EXPLANATION OF WHAT YOUTH WORKERS DO, WHY AND HOW

Introduction

These days everybody claims to be doing youth work. In response to the agenda set by *Every Child Matters*, *Youth Matters* and *Care Matters* youth workers are evolving into local multi-agency teams, pooling budgets and integrating their processes to treat more holistically the needs of young people. As they do so, the case is being made to recognise and reward the distinctive contribution of youth work. At national level, the same arguments are being advanced as government considers its priorities in developing a ten-year strategy for children and young people. Meanwhile the media relentlessly demonise the young and think tanks point to years of policy failure. In all the meetings and discussions about policy the very practice which forms the bedrock of youth work tends to get overlooked.

It is timely therefore to investigate the practice; to observe and explain how youth workers apply their skills. Ofsted reports these days tell us almost nothing about what youth workers actually do. Journalistic accounts tend to be superficial and theoretical pieces in academic journals can be arcane. While young people consistently testify to the difference youth work makes to them, the practice itself tends to remain unexplored.

This book describes and explains good youth work, drawing on the reflective practice of those who do it. It is aimed at practitioners and managers of youth work – wherever it is located in these days of integrated youth support services. And at policy-makers and commissioners who may want to know about the work they support. By examining what good youth workers do, we hope to make youth work practice explicit, visible and comprehensible; and thereby reveal its complexities, nuances and the different kinds of knowledge, skill, resource and insight that youth workers draw on in their everyday work. In doing so, we hope to illuminate what tends to be obscured by the much-used phrase 'the youth work approach'; and show how youth workers operate with sometimes very challenging young people in often difficult circumstances.

GOOD YOUTH WORK:

The recently published government ten-year strategy for positive activities for young people[1] emphasises the importance of structure and other key characteristics in provision. Research and evaluation studies have shown that if they are to be successful in engaging young people and enabling them to achieve, activities must, among other things, have a clear purpose and be facilitated by a trusted adult or older peer; the focus should be positive, focusing on developing skills rather than addressing deficits; they should address young people's needs in the round and encourage sustained participation.

These features are evident in the various examples that are described in this book. Yet good youth work will not be secured simply by ensuring that a checklist of key features is provided for. Over and above all else, it is enlivened and enriched by sets of relationships between adults and young people and among the young people themselves based on positive mutual regard and trust; and a sense that young people are an asset to their communities that should be protected, nourished and developed.

Good youth work is also stronger when it is approached as essentially an educational process in which the young people learn. There is continuing debate within the sector about the nature and methods of learning and whether and how it might be captured, 'measured' and accounted for. Yet good youth work occurs when those who practise it have a view about how young people learn. That is why the concept of curriculum, contested though it is, remains important and why texts[2] on the subject are worth revisiting.

This book is based on evidence collected from visits to youth work sites to observe the interventions as they took place and listen to the testimony of those involved. The youth workers were identified on the advice of experienced professionals. They were randomly selected and are by no means representative of the whole sector. The majority were women and located in the south and midlands of England but this does not mean that there are not as many good male youth workers situated in other parts of the country. I would like to take this opportunity to thank them for letting me see their work and for talking to me so openly about it.

The process was straightforward: direct observation of the youth worker (and the team) in operation, with the principal focus on the interactions between the youth worker and the young people and between the youth worker and other members of the team. A session would last anything from one to three hours. This would be preceded by a short conversation with the youth worker about the work that had been planned and its context; and would be followed by a longer interview either face-to-face or, if that were not possible, on the telephone. In this interview the youth worker reflected on what had happened during the session and explained why particular judgments and interventions had been made. In addition, some of the youth workers sent written explanations and accounts that further elaborated their approach and its underpinnings.

It is hoped that this book may serve as a timely reminder that the answers to simple questions such as 'what works?' require careful thought and analysis rather than instant responses. It is intended to inform discussion and debate at different levels about the nature and impact of the interventions youth workers make, the standards they aspire to, and their professional formation and development.

The 3 (or 4) Rs

There is a symmetry running through youth work that is sometimes missed by those who practise and preach about it. The very qualities and characteristics that the processes of personal and social development are intended to generate in young people are the same as those that youth workers aspire to and require if they are to be effective.

I refer to the three Rs of:
- **resourcefulness** – digging deep inside and outside one's self to find and use resources that help to respond to life's opportunities and risks;
- **resilience** – bouncing back from disappointment and setbacks in the pursuit of aspirations; and
- **resolve** – sticking at things, sometimes in adversity, to achieve goals.

In youth work these three Rs are secured through developing a fourth. **Relationships** of trust and mutual respect are the currency of youth work through which young people receive the support and challenge needed to acquire the 3 Rs. These qualities and characteristics are essential if opportunities and risks are to be recognised, assessed and taken.

Resourcefulness

Resources lie both inside and outside ourselves, a product of genetic and environmental factors. We draw on them all the time to help us achieve our purposes. In combination they enable us to achieve fuller lives. They tend to be distributed unevenly within families and communities. Public policy is deployed to compensate those who have less in attempts to create a fairer society.

GOOD YOUTH WORK:

Resources in themselves are of limited value if people do not have the capacity to use them. This entails recognising what they are, where they exist and employing wit and initiative in exploiting them. We learn how to do this in different ways, principally by closely observing those who can. This quality we might call resourcefulness.

It is reasonable to suppose that if young people can develop their resourcefulness, their life prospects will be enhanced. One way of doing so is to draw on people who are more experienced and adept and who can provide guidance and support in dealing with the kinds of challenges faced in growing up. In the world of youth work the term used to describe this process is peer mentoring.

> **Jane** is a community tutor at a secondary school in Tonbridge. She is found in Hut 9, the base for a peer mentoring scheme. It is a highly visible location and there is a continuous flow of school pupils in and out of the building during the day.
>
> In the scheme there are 30 peer mentors who are taking part in one of two activities: a short training course developed and supported by Kent Safe Schools for Year 11 pupils, and a year long BTEC Intermediate Certificate for those over 16. Mentors are paired up with pupils from lower down in the school who need support, usually for problems they are experiencing in school, in particular bullying. There is a system of planned appointments of half an hour. Efforts are made to ensure that pupils in receipt of the support do not miss the same lessons each week, while their mentors tend to use their general study or free periods. Jane ensures there is close liaison with the year heads who have pastoral responsibilities and with the school's inclusion team and special needs coordinator.
>
> It is lunchtime. About a dozen Year 10 and 11 girls are coming to learn about peer mentoring from one of the more experienced mentors. He asks them to write down the qualities or characteristics they would look for in a person they wanted to confide in; and the characteristics of someone they felt they could not confide in. There is a lot of talking across the two clusters of tables they are seated at and it is hard to get them to settle to the task. Jane is on hand to get them focused and has to intervene with a number of 'listen up, guys'. It works. Eventually they focus on the task and start writing, still with occasional bits of banter. But they stick at it and have done enough by the end to have a piece of work they can include in their portfolios.
>
> Afterwards in conversation the peer mentor who led the session says he is getting a lot from the scheme. He likes being able to help other people. He can see the

increase in their self-confidence and he himself feels valued by the experience. He thinks that he is also becoming more self-aware, finding resources in himself and helping others more vulnerable find them in themselves. He says that conversations with Jane, who checks in with each peer mentor after each one-to-one session, have revealed aspects of his mentoring practice where he can improve.

Jane has a good rapport with the young people who use Hut 9. She treats them as mature and they behave responsibly, knowing there are boundaries and respecting them. They clearly value the space because it means they can chill out from the stresses and strains of daily school life. It is testimony to the value they accord the scheme that they are happy to give up their free time in the lunch break to do some 'work' for the award. For them, it is a very different kind of education. They are beginning to appreciate that providing support means more than befriending. It means being trusted, sometimes with confidential information, and that trust has to be earned. It is not enough to be a nice person but you have to demonstrate a set of attitudes, behaviours and skills that are going to enable the mentee to open up and disclose the information needed if support is to be given. Jane provides a consistent role model and the peer mentors pick up on her behaviours and use them to provide their mentees with the kind of focused attention they need if they are going to be heard and helped.

GOOD YOUTH WORK:

Vickie runs a Social Inclusion Project in a youth centre in Solihull for Year 10 and Year 11 pupils excluded by schools and referred by local personal advisers and education welfare officers. She is helping four girls prepare for a presentation they are to make to another group of excluded pupils about a residential week-end they had taken part in earlier in the year.

The girls arrive on time and enter the room in good spirits. They are open, friendly and spend about twenty minutes talking about this and that with Vickie and her colleague Angie. They do not seem to be the slightest bit put out by having a visitor in the group. When they are reminded of the task they have to do, they begin to talk enthusiastically about their residential, recalling particular experiences as well as the feelings they had before, during and after the event. They clearly had enjoyed themselves and had moved beyond their respective comfort zones to take on new challenges – physical, emotional and social.

Vickie had prepared herself well for this session, bringing in card, felt-tip pens, and sundry materials for the girls to use to make their presentation, as well as printed photographs and pieces of flipchart paper which provided an excellent record and reminder of what they did on the residential and what they had felt about their experiences at the time. These materials were used by the girls to help arrange the points they wanted to convey in their presentation under the headings; what we did, what we felt, what we learned and achieved.

The girls set to the task well. They were focused and had plenty of ideas and impressions to share. They listed the kinds of activities they had taken part in, such as long walks, abseiling and various teamwork challenges. They recalled that beforehand they had felt nervous, anxious, excited, curious and scared to leave the family home; and that afterwards they had felt happy, relieved, sad (at leaving), more confident, proud of what they had achieved, closer to each other and excited to tell others about their experience. They had learned new skills (eg abseiling) and strengthened existing ones – communication, problem-solving, teamwork. And they had enjoyed each other's friendship.

Throughout the session, Vickie approached the girls respectfully and sensitively. She was also prepared to challenge, for instance at one point where one of the girls in her enthusiasm to tell her part of the story kept interrupting her friend. When Vickie pointed this out gently but firmly, the girl acknowledged what she had done.

These examples illustrate how youth workers effectively lead by taking an enabling role. They create the conditions and provide the materials for young people to develop their own skills and insights. They give young people the confidence to express their own ideas in ways they feel comfortable with. And in their relationships with young people they model befriending, showing that this entails both support and challenge, sometimes holding up a mirror so that young people can see themselves more clearly.

Resourcefulness also involves reflection, the ability to stand back and think about experiences, trying to distil the learning points and use them when faced with similar situations. By displaying in low-key fashion these skills – leadership, communication, befriending and reflecting – youth workers give young people the inspiration and confidence to try them out for themselves in a safe environment where they feel able to take risks.

Resilience

Effective youth work provides the protective factors needed for young people to develop resilience. This is required for navigating the choppy waters of adolescence. For a persistent number of young people school is a site of risk and vulnerability where bullying in the classroom and the playground can occur. This has always been the case to some extent but the problem appears to be increasing, predictably given the pervasiveness of bullying in other parts of our culture – the workplace, the street and on television 'reality' programmes where put-downs and ritual humiliations are offered as nightly entertainment.

> In a local youth centre in Canterbury, **Kyla** is coordinating a personal, social and health education session on bullying for a small group of Year 10 and 11 pupils who have been excluded from local schools. Kyla opens by asking what bullying is and with a positive contribution from one of the pupils identifies three types: physical, verbal and mental. The types that the young people say they are most familiar with are name-calling and being ignored or excluded from a group. Kyla then hands out 'agree/disagree' cards which the young people are asked to raise in response to a series of questions or statements such as 'if someone hits you, it's okay to hit them back'. The young people say this is like primary school but comply with the task. Most of the questions suggest a conditional response 'it depends'. One of the girls recognises this and consistently holds up both cards. Some of the boys appear not to think about their answer and raise the same card as their neighbour seated alongside. In the exchange that follows, one of the boys makes a

disparaging remark towards one of the girls for which he is challenged by Kyla.

There then follows a short activity where the group is given a hand-out on Maslow's hierarchy of needs and asked to write on it, for their files, how they think they would react if each level of need (physiological, safety, belonging, esteem) were not met. When one of the girls refuses to do this (because she misunderstood what she was asked to do and wrote something else on the hand-out), she is told that she will have to do it later. When completing the task, one of the boys replies 'I would kill myself' – a phrase he repeats two or three times during the session as well as disclosing that he had messed up an attempted suicide when he had been younger. This is noted by Kyla but not picked up at the time.

The group then watches an extract from a DVD made by another group of young people from the Kent Youth Service concerning text-bullying. They are asked to share their reactions to what they have seen. This leads to an exchange of views and name-calling; there is fair bit of winding-up between some of them. Kyla and one of her colleagues deal with it firmly but in a low-key way, making it clear that they cannot work with such disruption going on. At different points, Kyla challenges racist remarks and has to remind people not to 'get personal'. One of the boys is taken out of the room for a short period to cool off. There is also an instance when one boy challenges another constructively for not answering the question correctly. (Instead of saying *how* he would have *felt* in a given situation he describes *what* he would have *done*). After they have completed their worksheets the group are rewarded with a short 15-minute break outside before returning to other activities – art, English – in smaller groups.

This example shows how demanding even a relatively short episode of youth work can be. The young people created a stressful dynamic and tested the youth worker's ability to control a volatile situation. At various times the youth worker's comments seemed to be ignored. It would be normal to feel put down by this but it is important not to show it for that would be interpreted as a sign of weakness. It is equally important not to be provoked by a riposte designed to humiliate. As often these verbal missiles are directed towards other young people as to the youth workers. Losing face is to be avoided at all costs. Sometimes it seems as though the main driver of the young people's behaviour is to get their retaliation in first. The trick is not to show any sense of being hurt nor respond to having your 'buttons pushed'. The youth worker has to appear to operate above the fray without losing touch with the protagonists. Recovery from these ritualised bouts of mutual goading has to be quick and emphatic to be effective. Resilience is all.

AN EXPLANATION OF WHAT YOUTH WORKERS DO, WHY AND HOW

Resolve

Youth workers find themselves frequently working with young people who either have been excluded from school or are on the verge of being so. The trigger that leads to the exclusion is often an outburst of disruptive and anti-social behaviour by a pupil who becomes frustrated by the social and learning difficulties they experience in the classroom. They may not obtain the individual attention and encouragement they need to stick at a task they find challenging and so give up on it, demonstrating a lack of resolve. Referrals to an alternative curriculum project can mean an opportunity to start again in a less pressured environment where they can receive the individual support they need from a youth worker able to establish a rapport with them.

> **Lorraine** is one of a small team of youth workers who work alongside trained teachers at a project located in a refurbished youth centre in the centre of Derby. The project provides alternative education programmes for about twenty Year 10 pupils who have been excluded from school and referred on by local Pupil Referral Units (PRUs) because they need the special attention and support that the combined team can provide. Some of the pupils have behavioural conditions (eg ADHD and Tourette's) that create acute learning difficulties. The young people come through the project each week at different times and they are enrolled for a year's programme. Most attend for either a morning or afternoon and each half-day consists of three forty-minute sessions interspersed with breaks of about twenty minutes. The curriculum comprises English, Maths, Science, IT, Humanities and PSHE. The youth work team is responsible for delivering the last three.
>
> Lorraine is taking a boy for an IT session. He has ADHD and is apparently on new medication which he is still adjusting to. He finds it very difficult to concentrate for long. She sets him a task, word processing a piece of text for his AQA entry level certificate. It concerns life in the trenches during the first world war. He shows no interest in the content, simply in completing the task as soon as possible so he can have some time at the end to play a computer game – the reward for his effort.
>
> He works slowly, using a single finger on the keyboard, and makes mistakes. Surprisingly perhaps, these do not seem to frustrate him unduly. However, after ten minutes his attention begins to wander and he seems to tire of the task. Lorraine gently encourages him to keep going. He now intermittently asks to stop so he can play, but Lorraine is gently firm with him and says she expects him to finish. About half way through the lesson she moves to sit closer to him. She actually uses the keyboard to correct some of his mistakes. She can tell he has completely

GOOD YOUTH WORK:

lost interest in the task. With about three lines left to finish the copying, she lets him play the game. He has about five minutes before the session ends and he leaves in reasonably good humour. Lorraine says the important thing is that he will come back. She believes there is no point in forcing him to do something he has no interest in; and that, if she were to, he would leave in a bad mood and probably not return.

What is important here is that the youth worker recognises the boy's limitations and does not push him to the point of no return. He has shown sufficient resolve during the session to reap some reward for his efforts. He recognises that there is benefit in sticking at something he finds difficult. Next time he may be motivated to complete the task he has been set.

These examples of practice also show that youth workers are required to display the very characteristics they are trying to engender in the young people. During the sessions their resourcefulness, resilience and resolve are tested by the young people's attitudes and behaviour. They demonstrate patience and tolerance and always appear to be in control of the situation without making that feel oppressive. There is almost a tacit agreement between the young people and the youth workers that there will be some degree of challenge but never to the point that risks undermining the youth worker. At some perhaps unconscious level even the most demanding young people recognise that the authority of the youth worker provides a secure framework within which it is safe to test themselves and take risks.

Opportunities and risks

There is a growing consensus among policy makers and social commentators that globalisation, an essentially economic process that has extended and integrated global markets, has far-reaching social effects the meaning and implications of which we are beginning to grasp. One of these has been considerable impact on the economic structure and more specifically the youth labour market in Britain with consequent results for broader social processes including transitions to adulthood. Globalisation entails greater competitiveness and that brings new opportunities, such as a widening and extension of further and higher education, though not without direct costs; and risks which have at the same time both spread more widely across the population and intensified among particular groups. It has led to the embrace of consumerism across the world; and to government policies that seek to apply this pattern of consumption to public services – what has been referred to in some quarters as 'the personalisation of the public realm'.

What has this got to do with youth work, a modestly resourced public service accustomed to being treated as marginal by policy-makers and public alike? A great deal, since it lies right at the heart of the interaction of 'agency' and 'structure' that influences the choices made by young people during transitions. Globalisation simultaneously constrains and opens things up so that the experience of growing up in the contemporary world has become one of seeking and then navigating individual pathways, while avoiding or trying to overcome obstacles and pitfalls posed by structures, both established and emerging.

If the primary purpose of youth work is to foster the personal and social development of young people, then that means attending to both their aspiration to make the most of opportunities and their need to be protected from risks. Youth work provides positive activities that extend and enrich young people's experience and skills and safe places where they can influence and take part in such activities and enjoy the friendship of their peers. These are commonly offered in open access youth centres located in neighbourhoods, sometimes free-standing and sometimes as part of a school or complex of social facilities. The challenge for the youth worker running this type of facility is to:
- create an attractive environment to which young people want to come and a programme in which they choose to take part;
- manage a team of part-time staff so they can provide a selection of activities that are inherently enjoyable and through which young people can learn and achieve; and

GOOD YOUTH WORK:

- ensure that relationships between youth workers and young people and among the young people themselves are open, trusting, supportive and mutually respectful.

Carol is the area youth worker for Maidstone and responsible for the town's only full-time youth centre, situated in the middle of a large 1950s social housing estate. People have lived here for generations and have very low expectations and aspirations for themselves and their families. They are predominantly white, working-class although many are not working. When Carol arrived the youth centre was in a dreadful state and dominated by some very aggressive older lads who were not interested in doing much other than hanging around, smoking and causing trouble. The youth workers were not much better. Carol had to work hard to shift expectations and impose her own high standards. In doing so she met opposition from the users and some of the staff. She was determined to make a difference and persevered despite being physically attacked on two separate occasions. She won the support of some of the local residents and the local police.

Carol has had to struggle hard to lift standards in the club and make it into a place that young people want to attend. She has had little help from parents and finds many of their attitudes hard to accept. Some are racist, homophobic, into petty crime and drug use and have very little respect or understanding of people who are different. They seem fatalistic about their situation and do not encourage their children to raise their sights.

Carol says that she has learned most about her youth work from listening to, observing and understanding young people. She watches closely their behaviour and learns what motivates and upsets them and takes their attitudes and behaviour as clues to determine how to intervene. She seems to recognise much of herself in them, realising that she was much like them when she was young. She draws on her own experience all the time.

She is extremely well organised and has unusually high energy levels. Her determination and enthusiasm are infectious and she seems to bring out much the same qualities in the young people and the staff she works with. This results in high-octane youth work.

She also believes in planning. She believes that it is important to have a programme clearly set out in advance for each month and she involves the young people in establishing what that is. During the planning stage there is a flip chart on display each evening the club is open for young people to see how the programme is shaping up and to set out and offer their own ideas. During every session there is something set out on each table, indicating what the activity or topic is and each of the part-time youth workers on duty is deployed to be responsible either for a part of the building or for supervising a particular activity,

From the outside the club is distinctly unprepossessing. It is situated in an enclosed area at the edge of a large open space, surrounded by council houses. It is a single-storey purpose-built centre with a large recreational area, a sports hall, office, activity rooms and recently an extension has been added to create more activity rooms.

The standard of cleanliness and maintenance that has been established is most impressive. Every piece of furniture is in good condition, the place is spotless and everything is in its right place. It gives an impression of calm and order. But it also has life. There are displays of information everywhere and they are attractive and up-to-date. On entering the club the first display to catch the eye is a montage of photographs of the staff working with young people, with each of them having their specialist duties made clear. On different notice boards there is information about events going on in the area, the programme on offer in the club, forthcoming attractions in the county, policies and procedures, and information about education, careers and health. There are displays about particular issues affecting young people, such as bullying. The environment is stimulating, attractive and clearly focused on young people.

It is half past six in the evening and although the club does not open for a further half an hour some of the young people are already gathering outside the main entrance. The part-time youth workers begin to arrive. They chat briefly with Carol, checking out what they will be doing over the evening. One will be in the sports hall supervising ball games and badminton, one will be in the coffee bar, another in the kitchen making pancakes (it is Shrove Tuesday), another supervising the recreational area.

Carol is everywhere, and in the early part of the evening is being badgered from all sides by young people wanting keys to open doors or cupboards, equipment, materials or information. The shout 'Carol' can be heard from all corners of the club. She is quick and focused in her responses, apparently able to deal with several requests at the same time as keeping an eye and an ear out for anything she regards as untoward: bad language, an aggressive or unsympathetic remark, selfish behaviour, a risk to health or safety.

GOOD YOUTH WORK:

After a hectic start, Carol sits herself down for about twenty minutes at a table which has been set out for an activity concerned with relationships, the theme for this month's programme. She asks those young people who are sitting with her to explain what they think somebody 'cheating' on another means; she asks those passing by to write on a scrap of paper what they think is important in any relationship. Some youngsters draw or write their thoughts down, others take it frivolously and say things to shock or surprise – eg watching porn is seen by one member as 'cheating', by another as giving you ideas on how to behave with your partner! The young people are perhaps not yet mature enough to regard this seriously in front of their peers. They make sweeping generalisations that are challenged but they do not want to stay very long on the topic or the activity and quickly move on to something else in the club, or get distracted by one of their friends. Despite this, Carol is able to gather a fair number of remarks and ideas and at the end of the evening assembles these under headings and begins to discuss with some of the other youth workers how to take this forward with another activity in the club. This is done on the hoof, with people moving in and out of the conversation as they are doing other things or helping to clear up.

There are over fifty young people in this evening, mostly aged between 10 and 15. There are more boys than girls but they do not dominate, except in the sports hall. There is a lot of noise, some good-natured horseplay but little aimless running about. It is a bit like an indoor playground, with little clusters of young people in friendship groups, forming and re-forming for particular purposes or activities. Nobody seems to be on his or her own. Although there is the usual banter, there are no incidents of unpleasant, spiteful or bullying behaviour.

Conversations between young people and youth workers are essentially transactional and instrumental, with young people asking for things or youth workers giving or seeking information. No conversation seems to extend beyond a minute or two. The youth workers are stretched to keep activities going in a fairly purposeful way with a large number of boisterous young people in a relatively confined space.

This is a typical example of open access youth work, although, as organised, there is too much noise and activity to allow for any sustained group work or educational interventions. The centre provides a safe and secure environment for developing friendships and having fun. All are included, including a couple of older young people who appear to have learning difficulties. Relationships are open and youth workers seem well liked and respected.

AN EXPLANATION OF WHAT YOUTH WORKERS DO, WHY AND HOW

Carol herself is the focus of much attention. She is blessed with a loud voice which she uses from time to time to make announcements. But more than that she has a commitment and determination to provide for high standards. Her expectations are clear. She challenges any instances of infraction of the house rules (eg bad language) in a totally unthreatening way and the young people comply. She is as quick in thought as she is in deed; but then she needs to be able to keep on top of the process. In this way she can ensure that she and her staff provide young people with the opportunities they want to take part in positive activities; and to be listened to so their views are taken seriously. As a consequence they achieve outcomes (recorded and accredited) and a sense of belonging and being valued.

This session demonstrates the youth worker's skill of multi-tasking, of being alert and responsive to events as they occur while simultaneously seeking to shape them. Clarity of thought, word and deed and focus of attention tend to be casualties when under pressure to respond, provide and stimulate all at once. At first glance it may appear hard to detect whether and where there is any locus of control in the session. But it becomes evident that most of the lines of communication and energy are directed to and from the senior worker, not by virtue of her role and position, but by the sheer strength of her personality, skills of communication and dedication to the young people she works with.

GOOD YOUTH WORK:

Opportunities are offered and risks negotiated in other youth work settings too. For those young people who are not attracted to buildings but who prefer the open streets and spaces, detached youth work is the most commonly adopted approach. This is sometimes referred to as outreach work where the purpose of the intervention is to make contact with young people, inform them of opportunities that may be available in centres, clubs and projects and encourage them to take part. At the same time the youth workers befriend, advise and support those young people they meet on the street if and when it seems fitting.

> **Norman** does a couple of sessions of detached youth work a week in designated hotspot areas in Waltham Forest. There have been consistent calls from providers and users of local services for more positive activities and facilities for young people in these localities.
>
> This evening we meet up at a café with his colleague Abi in the high street by Walthamstow Central underground and bus station and at about 6pm we begin walking through the wet streets towards one of the hotspots – a block of flats. On the way we look out for young people in the streets and local play park but they are conspicuous by their absence. En route Norman and Abi talk about whom they expect to meet and what they want to do during the evening, as well as exchange information about particular young people they have been thinking about or in contact with since they last worked together.
>
> There seem to be three purposes to this coming session:
> - to reinforce existing contacts and make some new ones;
> - to inform young people about particular activities that are being planned with them in mind; and
> - to collect some disposable cameras from some of the young people who have been lent them with the purpose of taking photographs of things they like and do not like in their neighbourhood.
>
> When we reach the flats we mount the stairwell that has been identified by local people as one where the most anti-social young people hang out. The area is the subject of a dispersal order but there is no sight, sound or smell (of skunk) of young people in the vicinity. Perhaps the dispersal order is working or perhaps the imminent televising of an FA cup replay is keeping young people indoors.
>
> We leave the stairwell and walk through a courtyard to another and notice a small group of three young people idly kicking a football around. They are two girls aged

AN EXPLANATION OF WHAT YOUTH WORKERS DO, WHY AND HOW

15 and a boy aged 13, none of whom is known to Norman and Abi. The youth workers approach the young people explaining who they are, what they do and that they want to talk with them. The young people seem relaxed, friendly and open, though naturally a little shy since they have not seen these youth workers before.

The young people are asked if they are frequently out and about and say that they come out to play football. They report that it is safer here now than it used to be in the summer when there were evidently some troublesome young people about. When asked what activities they would like to do, they indicate an interest in football, basketball and paint-balling. Norman asks if they might be interested in an oral history project due to get under way the next day designed to create better understanding between the generations: young people and older people in the area will talk about how things used to be for young people and how they are now. The three young people politely decline the offer.

At this point a mother appears on one of the surrounding balconies and asks if the young people are okay. Norman and Abi point out that they are youth workers but the mother stays watchfully at a distance. Norman then asks the young people if he can take their names and phone numbers so he can keep them informed about activities coming up for local young people. For example, they seem interested in taking part in some scheduled workshops about sex and relationships. Norman proves to be a walking directory of different activities that the young people might be interested in doing and provides them with information about a range of possible venues. The young people seem grateful and pleased with the contact. They go back to their kick-about and we move on ...

... to the stairwell at the bottom of a low-rise block of flats, deemed to be the second hotspot, where a small group of girls aged about 16 is hanging out. They seem animated and are interested in the sex and relationships workshop that is mentioned soon after Norman and Abi greet them. When asked what they would like to learn and talk about and how the groups might be formed, the girls suggest a combination of single sex and mixed groups. They do not have any particular suggestions for subject matter but nod their heads in agreement when Norman and Abi go through a range of possible topics. Only one is interested in the oral history project and she takes a consent form when a third youth worker, responsible for organising it, arrives on the scene about ten minutes later.

Then some lads appear. One who seems a bit older than the rest says he has heard about the offer of free driving lessons from some agency trying to get people into

GOOD YOUTH WORK:

work. He is given the chance to sign up for them. Two of the boys are pretty stoned and they have huge joints. One of the boys tells Norman about a frustrating day he has had at work. Information is exchanged to see if any of the boys might be interested in any of the activities that are on offer. When asked, one of them goes back to his flat to retrieve the camera he has borrowed and returns it to Norman.

During this session youth workers have done a number of things. They have established or renewed contact with young people. They have been engaged in a process of mutual exchange of information. They have offered young people opportunities to extend their experience by taking part in new activities. They have picked up insights into the issues that concern the young people and they store these for future reference. They have shown that they are comfortable in the spaces young people choose to occupy and are not put off by some of their more eccentric behaviours. Thereby they earn young people's trust and confidence. They pay serious attention to what young people say and approach them with respect and a robust sense of humour.

A safe place

Youth centres and projects provide a **safe** environment. Young lives can be blighted by fear of failure, pressure to conform, and by physical, mental and sexual abuse. Some young people are witness to daily acts of petty and sometimes serious violence and it can take different forms. Good youth work offers a sanctuary where fears can be expressed and explored; and some of the 'taken-for-granted' norms of abuse in the family home can be challenged.

> **Jeanette** runs a youth centre on the southern outskirts of Rotherham that is well equipped and furnished to a high standard in a very modern style. Half an hour before the start of the session the team of three part-time workers arrives for a preparation meeting with Jeanette. Each has a clearly specified area of responsibility for the evening associated with the four main activities that take place each session: craft, cooking, sports and issues. The 'issue' this evening is to be domestic violence (a display on the wall shows photographs of women media celebrities made up to portray themselves as victims of physical abuse) which Jeanette wants to introduce as a taster with a short 'play'. The craft table is set up for making decorations for Chinese New Year. The kitchen area will be used for preparing fresh fruit and melted chocolate as part of the 'five a day' healthy eating programme. The fourth member of the team has more of a roving assignment. A sports instructor will be coming in at 8 o'clock to oversee an hour's sports activity session in the sports hall downstairs.
>
> The young people arrive as the doors open at half past six. They are mostly Year 10 pupils from the neighbouring school. Numbers are expected to be low because this week they have all been involved in work experience but within a quarter of an hour the numbers are rising to twenty. A small group of boys sits down by a large television screen and start playing a computerised football game. They also control the music. The girls sit in various clusters around the main area, with a particular group at the craft table with one of the workers By seven o'clock when the 'play' starts the number has swelled to 28, about an even number of boys and girls.
>
> 'Brian' comes back from work after a hard day and abuses his wife 'Mary' for looking drab and leaving the house in a mess. He is aggressive, demanding and insulting, making it clear that it is not Mary's job to think but to do as she is told, such as get him his tea. At a point where he is about to hit her, Jeanette who is supervising the activity stops it and invites the 'actors' to go through it again and asks those watching to stop the scenario at any time they want to alter Brian's

GOOD YOUTH WORK:

behaviour. Before doing so, she asks them to indicate where they think the power in the relationship lies.

The scene is acted out a second time, on this occasion with frequent interruptions from the audience, mostly the girls, although one boy in particular is very quick to point out where Brian is behaving badly. Again at the end Jeanette asks them to indicate where the power lies and this time it is more evenly balanced.

Jeanette makes it clear that this scenario was intended to advertise a ten-week programme on domestic violence that will be taking place in the centre over the coming weeks. Most of the girls say they are interested in taking part. It will draw on a pack of ideas and materials devised by a women's refuge in Leeds and will lead to an accredited award. A few minutes later, Jeanette is in discussion with a small group of younger boys who also express an interest but want to do it at a time when they will not be noticed by the older boys.

But violence and aggression sometimes erupts within the safe environment of the club or centre and it is important that the youth worker is alert to its imminence and able to nip it in the bud. For if the project or centre is not a safe place it forfeits its claim to provide a service for young people. Good youth workers are able to call on their experience and professional intuition to defuse such situations.

Kyla reports
'Many of our clients have a history of aggression and some violence. These young people have to be very closely monitored and their individual triggers noted. Conflict and aggression can arise almost spontaneously and acting on instinct and intuition (with the aid of experience) can help prevent a situation or deflect an incident. Whether it is intuition or sub-conscious prior experience based on information and past history that makes me aware of an issue arising or awareness of the individual's triggers, the important thing is to reduce the risks and remove the threat.'

A reflective space

Good youth work settings are also **reflective** spaces. In Kolb's cycle of experiential learning, there are four processes that should take place in sequence: experience, reflection, analysis, planning. When working with young people who tend to be action-oriented it is tempting when under pressure for the youth worker and the young people to miss out on the reflection and analysis and move directly from (one) experience to planning (the next). It can be difficult to persuade animated young people, excited by a particular experience, to pause and reflect on what they have gained from it and why; or to think about an event or incident that has happened and try and draw conclusions from it which can be applied in other settings. Good youth workers make time for this. By according it priority the intention is that the young people may also.

At a youth centre in Rayleigh in Essex, **Wendy** was introducing a group of girls to a new youth worker who was promptly told by one of the girls that she would find it difficult to last there. This prompted an unplanned discussion in the group about the behavioural norms among members and why young people can be so difficult to control. In turn this led to a discussion concerning the characteristics required to be a good youth worker in the centre.

A large piece of lining paper was rolled out on to the floor and one of the centre members was asked to lie on it. The young people used marker pens to draw an outline of her body, discussed the subject and placed the sought-after characteristics on the paper. Wendy led the discussion which was characterised by considerable self-awareness and insight; everybody took part.

The key characteristics they listed included:
- Respect by the youth worker towards young people and for the youth worker from young people.
- Friendliness.
- Trustworthiness – which led on to some interesting exchanges about the duty of youth workers to pass on information if they suspect a young person may be being abused in some way.
- Being positive and happy.
- Able to banter.
- Listening and other communication skills.
- Providing a mixture of support and challenge.
- Fairness and not being judgmental.
- Enabling young people to make decisions.

This latter point led into an exchange between the young people and the youth workers about whether they wanted youth leaders or youth workers. They described the former as being more directive than the latter. The girls were unanimous in wanting youth workers, though they realised that, for their own safety and welfare, there may be times when the youth workers has to 'lead' more.

GOOD YOUTH WORK:

The discussion was mature and the exercise tackled seriously. The girls were commended by Wendy and her team for their concentration and focus. The girls offered the view that these would have been absent had the boys been there. In turn this led on to discussion about gender differences and leadership styles among young people. This was well managed by Wendy who helped the young women conceptualise and move beyond the bald assertion and generalisation that tend to feature in these situations.

Another group, another context but again time set aside for reflection, although in different circumstances.

Nigel has designed a social education programme called *Choices Choices* that is targeted at boys and designed to enable them to consider the relationship between attitudes, behaviours and their consequences and he uses this in much of his work with disaffected pupils. He has developed it not to change attitudes and behaviour but to 'facilitate understanding and analysis of personal and cultural narratives so that [the young men] can reflect on the sort of men that they are and choose the sort of man they want to be'.

The programme comprises 13 weeks of two-hour sessions of direct group work with boys and young men. The material is intended to cover a 90-minute period allowing for ice-breakers, energising activities and breaks for the remaining half an hour. The programme is underpinned by guiding principles that include:
- responding to oppressive attitudes and behaviour as they occur with anti-oppressive educational interventions;
- demonstrating power sharing between male and female youth workers;
- building trust based on young people choosing to take part in the programme;
- observing confidentiality;
- developing empathy;
- providing a safe and secure environment in which to explore masculinity
- helping young men avoid making negative judgments about themselves and making adverse comparisons with others; and
- using resources that relate to young people's experience.

It is a cold Monday afternoon in early February at a large comprehensive school on the outskirts of Coventry. Pupils are making their way back to classes after their dinner break. At the Multi-Agency Resource Area, the former house of the school caretaker, Nigel is planning a session with his co-worker Susie who manages a programme of support for pupils who are not thriving in school.

This is the eighth session of a weekly programme with six boys from Years 8 and 9 who have the worst attendance and the highest rate of detention in the school and who are periodically short-term excluded. They come into the room in ones and twos, some with their rucksacks and some without. They seat themselves around an oval shaped table. At one end sit Nigel and Susie.

They start the session with a 'round', asking each of the boys in turn to talk about something in the last week which has been negative for them and caused them stress. One boy mentions a fight he got into with a girl whom he did not hit back because he has a principle of not hitting girls – he comes from a family where he was often witness to his father beating up his mother. Another boy talks about his mother being in hospital with the result that he is now being looked after by his step-father. A third boy had spent a couple of days in the last week 'missing' having walked out of his home following a violent confrontation with his step-father. They then talk about positive things that have happened. This proves more difficult, although most of the incidents selected refer to achievements in sports of different kinds.

From this round, a short conversation strangely emerged in the group about people's right to die if they are suffering pain as a consequence of illness or accident. The boys seem interested in life and death matters and the right any individual has to end or prolong their life. There was some discussion about the reasons for legislation that disallows euthanasia.

Nigel later brings out large sheets of flipchart paper that have been kept in a roll. Each of these represents a timeline for one of the boys in which they have recorded key events that have happened to them in their lives. They do this as a means of reflecting on what has happened to them and how these events or experiences have had an impact. There is a common pattern with these; their parents breaking up not long after they are born, followed by their mother taking up with another or, over a period, a series of other partners; holidays, in some cases to far-away places; some encounters (good or bad) with a pet; early sexual intercourse (actual or claimed?); and short-term exclusions from secondary school at various points.

Over the session a lot of ground had been covered: feelings of stress and enjoyment; conflict and its resolution in school (and in Iraq); bullying, racism and stereotyping; what is regarded as 'typical' male behaviour and the pressures imposed on boys to be men of a certain type; choices and consequences; behaviour. None of this was explored in any depth but the boys were invited to offer their views and encouraged

GOOD YOUTH WORK:

at all times to listen to each other. They found it harder to listen than to talk, although overall they showed each other and the workers a measure of respect which they rarely do in relation to their peers and teachers in the conventional school setting.

It is hard to be clear about what they had learned from the session. They were not asked to comment on that at the end. But some clearly showed an impressive measure of self-control and tolerance towards others.

Reviewing what the boys have gained from each session is usually part of each session, and is recognised as part of the positive impact of being in the group. However, judging the appropriate time is challenging when working with a group of boys whose attention spans are variable and whose behaviours in a group can change dramatically within a short time. If a review of learning or what has been thought about is not conducted in a session, it will be emphasised in the review of the previous week's learning at the start of the subsequent session, using the notes taken during the session itself.

The use of the timeline is a regular feature of his sessions as well. Each week Nigel hopes the boys will add to this, deepening and extending their insight into their lives and helping them to accept, as a normal aspect of their experience, reflection on the past as a means of making sense of the present. He also recognises that sometimes they are not ready to do this and he never pushes the activity against their will. He introduces this and various other activities designed to encourage reflection as a means of giving the boys a greater sense of control over their behaviour.

Activity and achievement

Since the start of 2007 there has been a statutory duty laid on local authorities to secure and publicise positive activities for young people as means of promoting their personal and social development. This is to be done in collaboration with partners from the private and voluntary sectors. Through these activities young people are expected to enjoy and achieve, one of five outcomes being pursued by means of the *Every Child Matters* agenda. Youth work is regarded as having a major contribution to make to this policy priority. Good youth workers run programmes of activities that engage young people and provide gateways to achievement.

> A youth centre on the outskirts of Canterbury provides the usual range of indoor and outdoor activities found in open access youth work. Recently the programme has included 'Give it a Go', a means of giving young people the opportunity to record their participation and achievement through keeping a portfolio. Each activity has a number of tasks associated with it; for each task a number of points are awarded and these points can be redeemed for prizes – eg hair styling products and equipment, a DVD player. This seems to have given a number of young people the incentive to record their outcomes.
>
> This evening there are four part-time staff working alongside Justin, the full-time youth worker in charge. Jean does cookery behind the coffee bar and supervises two boys baking cakes. James supports two home-grown bands in succession in the music room; neither band has been playing long and both show considerable promise. Stuart oversees indoor and outdoor games. Nancy runs a dance session with a small number of boys and girls in the studio. Justin appears to have a roving brief and spends a fair bit of his time with two senior members planning the making of a film/video/DVD to promote the centre and its activities.
>
> Altogether between twenty and thirty young people drift in and out of the centre over a two hour period. Most of them are purposefully engaged in one or two activities. Occasionally a small group of high-spirited lads steps across the boundary and disrupts the activities and enjoyment of others and this prompts a firm but fair reaction from **Justin**, the full-time youth worker. Relationships all round are good. The young people are open, relaxed and generally friendly with each other, with staff and visitors. There is the occasional bit of banter and some unpleasant remarks made by one or two boys about another boy being 'gay' because he is taking part in the dance activity.

GOOD YOUTH WORK:

At the youth centre in Rotherham the attractive wall displays are a prominent feature and provide colourful and vivid testimony to the activities and achievements that the young people take part in. On one wall under the heading *Youth Work Curriculum* there are photographs of young people taking part in various activities inside and outside the centre – on a trip to Morocco, outdoor adventure as part of the Duke of Edinburgh's award scheme, healthy eating. On another is the club programme in three sections showing what is happening on each of the three nights that the club is running. On a third wall there is a brilliant display of stars, each one with a young person's name and an achievement inscribed upon it. On other walls are posters and information on ground rules and contracts for the centre, health and safety, and particular themes such as anti-racism. A study of the wall displays alone gives a strong indication of the range of activities that the young people are involved in and of the principles that underpin the work that goes on in the centre. The impression given is one of vitality, enjoyment and considerable achievement.

Jeanette recognises the importance of having achievements recognised both informally and formally. *'Accreditation enables young people to achieve while having fun and learning about themselves and the world around them. Local and Open College Network awards are brilliant for recording and recognising movement and growth. This is evident from the work I have done with young people who have been excluded from school. By recognising where these young people have come from and tailoring provision to their needs they then have ownership and a greater sense of self-worth. Recognising starting points is essential as it shows progression. For young people to have a sense of achievement and a future is vital for their well-being.'*

Choice and voice

Youth work stresses the importance of young people exercising choice and expressing their voice as part of their personal and social development. This is important because they are users of public services and user choice and voice are seen as vital in driving up standards. It is also important because part of growing up entails making decisions and taking responsibility for their consequences, both for oneself and for others. Youth centres and projects therefore become sites for young people's active involvement in decision-making. In some ways they are the standard-bearers and ahead of the game, demonstrating how to do it to other services for children and young people. Some local authorities have acquired beacon status for the work they have done in furthering young people's participation and influence in policy making at different levels.

Giving young people the opportunity to shape events is accorded high priority in Rotherham. **Jeanette** reports *'we endeavour to offer a range of activities so that young people then have the freedom of choice. Young people are given the opportunity at the beginning of a session to shape the provision at that time. The young people are also given the chance to give feedback to the staff team, utilising a feedback or comments sheet and diary. During the session, staff support young people in reflecting on their work giving them positive and constructive feedback. This is a two-way process and young people are invited to comment on the events in each session'.*

In the Rochford area of Essex, the district youth council used to be in the hands of well-adjusted, competent and achieving young people, effective in advocating on behalf of their peers in the district ... up to a point. But they were not representative. After a while three young men on mopeds arrived at the centre and asked to see 'the lady who we get the money from'. The money was the Youth Opportunity Fund (YOF) that they had heard about from a detached youth worker. These young men were 'gatekeepers to the area', known and knowing, wielding considerable influence over other young people in the district.

Wendy decided they would make an interesting nucleus for a transformed youth council, since they represent young people who are usually regarded as a bit beyond the pale – the disaffected, the non-joiners and under-achievers.

Some of the original 'safe' members have moved on but others have stayed. So the local youth council is now far more representative of the whole youth population than it was.

They meet once a fortnight. Each meeting is structured in the same way. At the start they have a formal agenda and 'do the business' and this lasts about as long as their concentration span – rarely for more than half an hour. Then they do an 'activity' which is more like a conventional youth work evening.

The youth council has formed three sub-groups. The first are representatives of the area on the Young Essex Assembly, the youth forum for the whole county; the second are involved in Youth Bank, dealing with grant applications from young people's groups administered through the YOF; and the third is doing 'research' commissioned by the Children's and Young People's Strategic Partnership on three themes that have been identified by the partnership: drugs, sex, bullying. The group is trained in different 'research' techniques and methods.

The youth council has met with senior officers, including the chief executive of the district council, to discuss various matters of concern to elected members, in particular anti-social behaviour. One of the meetings did not go well because the young people acted up a lot and youth workers had to intervene to alter the dynamics and achieve a better outcome. This has not put them off trying again and they have decided to have an evening called 'Dig your digs' (short for dignitaries) when they will host local people of influence and give them a chance to hear more about what young people in the district think about living there.

Responding to the here and now

One of the characteristics of work with young people is to regard them as in transition, as being on the path to somewhere else. This is an understandable assessment of their position. However, it does not take account of the way they themselves may see their own situation which is very much in the present. Their future status as fully paid up members of society with all the attendant rights and responsibilities may be of less importance than what is happening to them at the time. Adults tend to see adolescence as a phase people pass through rather than as a status in its own right which contains its own distinctive features.

Generally, we tend to regard adolescence as a phase of change, as a period of being 'in between' childhood and adulthood. This may not be helpful because it may mean that we have one eye on the past and the other on the future. Neither is on the present which is where the young person is located. We should perhaps focus on 'adolescenthood' in its own right, as argued over forty years ago by Henry Maier and others, because it marks a significant part of the life cycle. During this period the young person has an abiding interest in, among other things, relating the self to others and to the wider world. Young people's thinking begins to be concerned with 'fitting the pieces together', building a consistent whole out of their hitherto partially developed understanding of life experiences and ideas.

However, in microcosm the process of youth work reflects the general tendency to see young people as in a process of transition from where they are to somewhere else. It should not be surprising therefore that youth work attends to the personal and social *development* of young people, implying that young people are still in the process of becoming. Programmes and projects established by youth workers have outcomes (educational and social) in mind and are planned so that they can be achieved.

AN EXPLANATION OF WHAT YOUTH WORKERS DO, WHY AND HOW

Before a young person crosses the threshold of a club or centre, the team of youth workers will have established objectives for the evening and have marshalled their resources so that these can be achieved. The preoccupation with outcomes could mean that they cannot always be expected to be giving a 100 per cent attention to the here and now. In other words, the practice of youth work is a combination of planning and spontaneity, of intention and responsiveness. Sometimes the best laid plans have to be set aside to deal with more immediate concerns and priorities that the young people bring with them into the session.

Wendy says that the balance between planning and spontaneity can be struck if you are well aware of the needs of the individuals and groups you are working with; and if one is well prepared, willing to take a few risks and not afraid if things do not go exactly to plan.

> *'Recently while working with a small group, plans were to bring in photos of each other when we (youth workers and young people) were babies. This was off the back of a session addressing issues of identity and relationships. We had planned to have a fun ice-breaker 'guess the name of the baby' and build up to a more in-depth look at relationships particularly between young people and parents. As much as we tried with this, the session was bitty because some of the group were behaving in a challenging way and needed to be managed. Every time I went to engage with the young people who had brought photos in I'd start with ... and would have to say "hang on a minute" or "I'll be back I just need to sort this out". This was done in a respectful way by valuing and recognising the needs of the whole and although we did not achieve the in-depth work we did get to share 'baby stories' which were significant in building trust, having fun and developing relationships.'*

Jane also recognises that it is important to deal with what young people bring and take every opportunity to respond to needs and interests as they emerge even if they knock her plans for the session out of shape.

> *'Everything we do is planned ... because we consult with young people all the time, I feel that sometimes there's a bit of pressure on them to come up with ideas ... we do what we can to encourage them ... in the girls' and boys' project, it gets more intense ... the other night we had session planned (sexual health, making banners) but about five people wanted to see me on a one-to-one ... one girl in her 20s chatted and chatted and chatted and gave me her life story ... thought she was a bit obsessive, important to note if she was going to be a volunteer ...checking in is important, asking "where are you at, how are you doing, how has your week been?" '*

GOOD YOUTH WORK:

'I'm always plugging ... I'm straight in there with the information ... letting them know about the opportunities ... that word 'intense' comes back again ... I try not to miss a trick...when I'm in, I'm in ...'

Lorraine plans ahead in her youth work but also tries to be responsive. She thinks it is no good going ahead with your plan if the young people are clearly not going to respond. She gave an example of some recent neighbourhood youth work where she and her colleagues were concerned at the ways in which young people were playing with toy guns on the street, imitating behaviour they had seen on the screen. Lorraine was concerned that they would be picked up by the police if seen by local people unaware that they were only play-acting. She thought it important to bring the risks associated with this activity to the notice of the young people. She had planned how to do this but on the evening in question the young people were clearly in no mood to listen. So she sat down with them at the arts and crafts table and, while they were together doing some graffiti art, she brought the topic up discreetly in conversation, saying how scary it was watching them do this on the streets and pointing up some of the hazards. The young people readily engaged with the topic, picked up some useful learning points and some of them changed their behaviour accordingly.

AN EXPLANATION OF WHAT YOUTH WORKERS DO, WHY AND HOW

The qualities and skills of youth workers

The examples of practice cited in this book demonstrate how difficult it is to specify the qualities required for good youth work. Certainly the national occupational standards help to classify and codify the skills and attributes but barely do justice to that combination of art, craft and hard graft that is entailed in the kinds of imaginative, planned and reactive interventions that youth workers are making in their everyday contact with young people.

Knowing young people and understanding their situations, motivations, hopes, fears and dreams is an essential starting-point for good youth work. This is always important, but especially so when working with challenging young people. **Norman** believes his job is to help young people 'reframe reality', especially those who consistently trip up or get into trouble, and find themselves at the wrong end of the law or threatened with an ASBO or court appearance. This means asking them to think about what they want(ed) to achieve, reflect on their behaviour and consider whether the choices they make help them get what they want. He asks them a lot of 'what if ...' questions to help them consider alternatives and ways out of some of the negative patterns they have become trapped by.

Norman reflects a lot on his own behaviour as a youth worker. He is conscious that he does a lot of confronting and challenging as well as providing support and development opportunities. He knows that sometimes he behaves unwisely, perhaps getting angrier than he should. Yet he acknowledges his misjudgment or mistake and will apologise. He always seeks to give an explanation. Young people respond well to this. It helps to create those levels of trust and mutual respect that drive the kind of relationships needed for young people's personal and social development.

Self awareness is an important quality echoed by **Jeanette**.

> *'Knowing me, knowing you – is that an Abba song? is probably the most used skill and possibly the most important. What I mean by this is that 'knowing me ...' is about knowing yourself – self-awareness – before we know young people. Knowing what you are about enables you to work with young people as you reflect your attitudes, beliefs and experiences in the way you work ... and act as a vital role model for young people in an informal setting where we are freer to be ourselves than some other professionals. We all know that young people can spot people who are a fake. Keeping it real encourages young people to be themselves and engage in a positive relationship. Being able to laugh at yourself is a good starting point as if you don't young people certainly will." '*

GOOD YOUTH WORK:

Linda in Coventry refers to the qualities required when providing an open access youth centre offering multiple activities simultaneously with a wide range of interests, needs, ideas and aspirations.

> *'I think the skills I use the most are the ability I have to develop positive relationships, I rarely forget a young person's name. If I don't see them for five years, I still remember their name and lots of other things about them. I seek to be approachable, consistent [really important for some young people in their chaotic world] responsive, can mix and match methods and settings. I have a vast toolbar of ideas which I can use to respond to young people's changing needs and interests. I try to be honest, non-judgmental, able to challenge in a supportive way.*

> *'Being an experienced worker many of the situations that occur have happened before so the experience tells you what is likely to happen. With this knowledge your instinct is honed. I also think that there is a code of behaviour that reinforces all our work. It includes valuing young people, recognising yourself as a role model, always doing what you say you will, recognising and using both verbal and non verbal communication.'*

Accentuating the positive is regarded as essential by **Jane** too. She is *'... always picking out the positives, polishing the diamond and helping them to see that reflect on them ... a lot of it is bigging them up as well, however small, not ignoring the negative but saying that's not all that you're about ... I know that's not the real you, I am always aiming to see the real them inside ... my aim all the time is to bring the sparks out in their eyes ... try my hardest not to miss an opportunity to bring the positive out.'*

She also considers a sense of humour to be important. Not only is it highly valued by young people who use humour a lot to make themselves known and establish rapport but it also helps in keeping perspective and a due sense of proportion.

> *'The biggest thing is humour, I use it a lot and don't even think about it ... it helps diffuse situations ... there's a lot of it going on in school ... have to manage the boundary, though ... it's really keeping me going at the moment ...'*

Young people are stretching boundaries for much of the time – it is their way of exploring the world around them and also testing relationships. Finding an adult who can be trusted and befriended is unusual for many young people. Therefore it is understandable that, once found, the adult will be challenged to see whether they revert to the behaviours that young people tend to associate with adults, such as the arbitrary use of power and authority. The wise use of the authority acquired by age, status, experience and respect is a talent noted in good youth workers.

In the Alternative Curriculum Programme in Canterbury, despite being severely tested by the young people **Kyla** and her team appeared to be in control throughout. Certainly boundaries were being pushed but rarely crossed. And whenever they got close the young people were reined in by a timely, firm but fair intervention. There was only once a cause to take someone out to cool down. The young people seemed to feel safe with the environment, the activity and with each other, mainly because they were being properly 'contained'.

The use of group work skills was evident in **Nigel**'s work.

The boys engage in the conversation with varying degrees of enthusiasm and interest. It is clear from the start that two of them are not sure they want to take part. One complains frequently of having a headache and seeks excuses for leaving the room to get an aspirin or a glass of water. Another buries his face in his arms or instead makes irritating screeching noises to wind people up. This attention-seeking behaviour works to some extent but it does not distract Nigel from pursuing the themes of the session.

This week the conversation is concerned with the fighting and bullying that can accompany racist taunts. A link is made between violence among rival groups and individuals in school on the one hand and the insurgency taking place in Iraq on the other. One of the incidents the boys refer to was a fight that took place last year between a boy who was from a family of Iraqi refugees and a couple of boys in the school who had earned a reputation for being hard. The Iraqi boy had gained respect for his courage in defending himself and 'battering' the indigenous boys. His response was compared favourably by one of the group with that of the boy in the group who had chosen not to fight with the girl who had taunted and attacked him the previous week. This was probably intended to provoke a reaction but the second boy struggled – successfully – to restrain himself.

Nigel could see that the boy was becoming upset by the taunts so he invited him to move his chair and come and sit next to him. He cleverly engaged him in the conversation about bullying, encouraging him to turn his back on the other lad. When the protagonist realised that his disruptive behaviour was not going to derail the session, he decided to engage with the discussion, leaving his friend, who had been asking for aspirin and a drink since he arrived, alone. Eventually he too began to engage, in particular towards the end.

GOOD YOUTH WORK:

The session ended well, although the disruptive boy's intermittent winding-up of his peer had caused the latter to walk out of the room on one occasion. He was not stopped although as he left Susie asked if he would like to come back before the end of the session. He did.

At the end of the session he was congratulated by Nigel for some of the decisions he had made during the session: changing his place so he was seated beside Nigel when the winding-up persisted; leaving the room when it became too much; and returning when he had time to distance himself from the source of irritation and to compose himself sufficiently for re-entry.

Drawing on one's experience is something that youth workers do instinctively. **Lorraine** says that she understands where these young people are coming from and she uses her experience to understand them. A lot of her work is instinctive, learned responses from situations she has previously found herself in. **Vickie** also draws on her experience a great deal in her work – it is almost her stock in trade. She says she had a difficult period in her youth, becoming a single mother when young. She was later employed in the car industry where she led the all-male seat build section which she describes as 'an excellent preparation for youth work'. She is well versed in the ways of the young. She has a personality and approach that they warm to and is observant in her interactions so she notices when issues need to be picked up, either at the time or later on. She enjoys the combination of one-to-one casework and group work and is able to move the young people between the two types of intervention in ways that suit them best.

Good youth workers are not afraid to challenge young people and the assumptions they hold about the world they live in. This sometimes means confronting their attitudes and behaviour. They try to take the young people beyond the starting-point each time they work with them. **Wendy** says she would not practise her youth work in any other way.

'I think young people are much too underestimated and I try to challenge their development. It may seem 'simple' and 'obvious' to people looking in/on but to a young person struggling to maintain themselves in an appropriate way in a group – for them not to use abusive language as a matter of course is progress. The skill is defining the starting point and redefining the progress line, explaining the reasons for that starting point and acknowledging their progress in a respectful genuine way.'

AN EXPLANATION OF WHAT YOUTH WORKERS DO, WHY AND HOW

This final example illustrates how a good youth worker can convert a crisis into an opportunity, even in a situation when under great pressure. It reveals some of the qualities and skills required.

> At a secondary school on the outskirts of Coventry a group of Year 10 pupils had been finding it hard to manage a conventional timetable. For them the turning point was a residential held at an Outward Bound centre towards the end of their year. This was part of the Prince's Trust XL programme on which they were enrolled. **Amanda**, the youth worker, was accompanied on the trip by the school's head teacher who had persuaded the governors that it was in the school's interest that he should spend five days away with some of its most challenging pupils. Up to this time he had been very wary of youth work, his experience of it in the past having been uncontrolled young people in school-based youth centre premises out of school hours. He wanted to become better acquainted with the youth work process. He thought that as a qualified mountain leader his experience would be an asset.

GOOD YOUTH WORK:

Amanda was ambivalent about the head teacher's presence on the trip. All went well until the penultimate day of the residential, when the young people had to find their own way to an agreed point, equipped with a map, compass and two-way radio while the staff (Amanda, the head teacher and an instructor from the Outward Bound centre) tracked them from behind. At one point the group of young people started messing about and one of the boys went off with the map and another went off with the two-way radio, leaving the rest of the group without any means of finding their way or of communicating with the staff. However cometh the hour, cometh the man and one member of the group (who suffers from dyslexia, ADHD and Tourettes) emerged to lead the rest back safely to the arranged meeting-point.

The head teacher was cross and told Amanda that there would be 'consequences'. Amanda stood firm and said she would like to deal with the situation in a developmental way. In the evening, after the group had bathed, dressed and eaten, there was the usual de-briefing meeting and Amanda issued each member of the group with a small supply of post-its. On these she invited them to record what they had felt when the first member of the group had run off with the map, when the second had run off with the two-way radio and when the third had led them to safety. The comments made about the first two were very sobering. Group members said they had felt afraid, anxious, angry and helpless. Remarks about the third member were very different; they had felt relieved and grateful to him. He visibly grew in pride and confidence as he received their plaudits and has remained a lead figure in the group, taking responsibility for applying for money for an activity through the local YOF.

Both Amanda and the head teacher independently testified to the benefits of working in this way, of giving the young people themselves the chance to take responsibility for the consequences of what had happened. Its effect was to change the formation and dynamics of the group and for the young people to recognise that they were capable of resolving differences and solving problems. Since then the group has found the XL programme a safe, reflective space to deal with incidents and feelings; and to consider, explore and take up opportunities to achieve positive outcomes.

One of the key qualities in Amanda recognised by the head teacher on this trip was patience. When a young person baulked at the prospect of doing something, she would painstakingly explain the consequences and then give the young person time to make up their mind as to what to do. It was her commitment to the young person and her powers of persuasion that most impressed.

As a consequence of demonstrating these qualities, it is common for pupils who are struggling to cope with the demands and expectations of school to refer themselves to Amanda and her colleagues for guidance and support. When a pupil presents him or herself at the door of her office saying 'I'm on report and about to be excluded ...', Amanda has a routine which entails finding out where the hot spot areas of possible frustration and 'kicking off' are for the young person in the school, specifying areas in the curriculum where they are struggling, identifying what support may be needed from curriculum leaders, tweaking the timetable and finding a safe and secure place where they can do their work.

Amanda is also a powerful advocate for the rights of these young people. When previously a school has inadvertently failed to observe the regulations on 'excluding' a pupil for a short 'cooling off' period, Amanda has reminded the teachers about their obligations under the safeguarding legislation to inform the parents or carers in writing and ensure there is somebody at home to look after them. This has not always made her popular but teachers are now beginning to recognise and respect the contribution the youth workers make to the welfare, education and development of the children and young people in their charge. The head teacher believes that the school is probably making a bigger contribution to helping the children to achieve the five outcomes of *Every Child Matters* and *Every Young Person Matters* as a result of the efforts, skills, integrity and determination of the youth work team.

The head teacher consequently has very interesting views about the contribution of youth work. One of the strategic priorities of the school is to build social capital within the school and the wider community. This is because if the school, which is 'facing challenging circumstances' is going to move up a gear and improve its performance substantially, it is going to have to win over parents so they more actively support the school and their children's progress through it. Youth workers have proved adept at engaging some of the more challenging parents with education, even though in some cases they may at first be hostile to it and what it stands for – often their own failure and humiliation.

The head teacher now sees the value of youth workers 'living cheek by jowl with the school' and the youth work ethos running alongside the classroom ethos. He sees the two as complementary, not necessarily in conflict. And he sees Amanda and her colleagues as centrally involved in the regeneration of the neighbourhood because of what they are doing for the young people and their families. This has become something of a revelation for him.

GOOD YOUTH WORK:

Last words

This book has set out to explain what good youth workers do and demonstrate how they contribute to the wellbeing and development of young people. The work described is not exceptional. Indeed, it illustrates well the kinds of situation facing many youth workers as they get to grips with the emerging agenda. What hopefully has become clear is that good youth work is demanding because young people have complicated lives and many of them face most challenging circumstances.

To summarise, youth work essentially helps young people to develop **resourcefulness, resilience** and **resolve** through relationships with their peers, with youth workers and with other adults. Thereby they can respond more effectively to opportunities and risks.

The work is done in a supportive environment which provides time and space for young people to be
safe – from harm, hurt (emotional), fear, failure, pressure to conform;
reflective (of self and others) so as to think about the reasons for their situations and feelings; and the consequences of their decisions and actions; and
active by taking part in:
(a) conversations and discussions where they can express their views and
(b) activities which are fun, which they enjoy and through which they achieve.

Through youth work experiences and activities, young people make sense and meaning of their experience; and find their voices and make choices, accepting the consequences of both.

Youth workers are there **in the present**, in the here and now, taking young people as they are, on their terms and dealing with whatever they bring. Youth workers act in the interests of young people in the sense that they are:
(a) **trusted** because they listen attentively, befriend, offer confidence, do not judge, respond and reflect; they hold a mirror to young people's experience that provides perspective by both looking back to consider causes and antecedents and looking forward to anticipate consequences; and
(b) **adults** who
- ◆ inform, advise and signpost where appropriate;
- ◆ provide wise counsel;
- ◆ advocate on behalf of;
- ◆ support;

AN EXPLANATION OF WHAT YOUTH WORKERS DO, WHY AND HOW

- ◆ challenge; and
- ◆ maintain boundaries.

To do this youth workers deploy a range of professional skills, knowledge and instincts and display the same characteristics they are seeking to elicit in the young people they work with. These are not easily come by. Indeed they are won by a combination of experience and training that stretches the mind and the imagination and asks questions that often have serious psychological, ethical and political implications.

Ultimately, youth workers make a stand alongside young people and, in doing so, occupy uncomfortable territory where continuity and change meet; where young people confront adults with their legacy with all its contradictions, imperfections and complexities; and rightly ask for something better. In seeking to strike a better deal for the generation coming through and in striving for a fairer society, youth work is essentially concerned with social justice. That is a prize worth winning.

GOOD YOUTH WORK:

1 *Aiming high for young people: a ten year strategy for positive activities*; H M Treasury and Department for Children, Schools and Families, 2007
2 For example
   Youth Work: Education Observed 6; Department for Education and Science; 1987
   The Youth Work Curriculum; Office for Standards in Education; Crown Copyright; 1993
   Towards a Contemporary Curriculum for Youth Work; Bryan Merton and Tom Wylie; The National Youth Agency; 2002
   Youth Work Process, Product and Practice; creating an authentic curriculum in work with young people; John Ord; Russell House Publishing; 2007